We are chicks. We are in the kennel with Wellington.

We are pecking

Wellington on his chin.

Peck, peck.

We are pecking Wellington on his cheek. Peck, peck.

Wellington gets cross.

'Get off me. Grrr....
Go away,' he says.

We all get off
Wellington. We all go
to look for the hen.

She is in the shed.

She is on the nest.

Oh no! She has laid an egg. She will sit on it for weeks.

We all go back to Wellington. He is a soft cuddly dog.